MOTORCYCLES THAT GO ZOOM! AND VROOM!

written by
T.D. RICKETTS

illustrated by
VEA LEWIS

DEDICATED TO

Terri, Sarah,
Auntie, Henry
and George
Hope you like it.
Thanks for the
encouragement.

Motorcycles have two wheels and there are many different kinds.
All kinds of people ride them.

Dirt bikes play in the mud
and jump hills.
Their riders wear all kinds
of protection.

Café racers go really fast.

They ride on roads.

Trials riders can climb stumps. They go slow and climb all kinds of stuff.

Custom bikes come in all shapes and sizes. Choppers have long front ends sticking out.

Baggers have all
kinds of trunks.
They go a long way
on the highway.

Cruisers just like to ride all over.

They are just happy to be riding.

Mopeds are a different type of motorcycle. They aren't as fast or as big as most bikes. You Can pedal them like a bicycle.

Scooters are like a motorcycle but not quite.
You can step through them.
A lot of kids really like scooters.

People that ride motorcycles
are called riders.
Some like to be called bikers.
There are all kinds
of clubs for riders.

Groups of riders do a lot of charity rides. They help raise money for people who need it.

They help sick people and veterans and shelters.

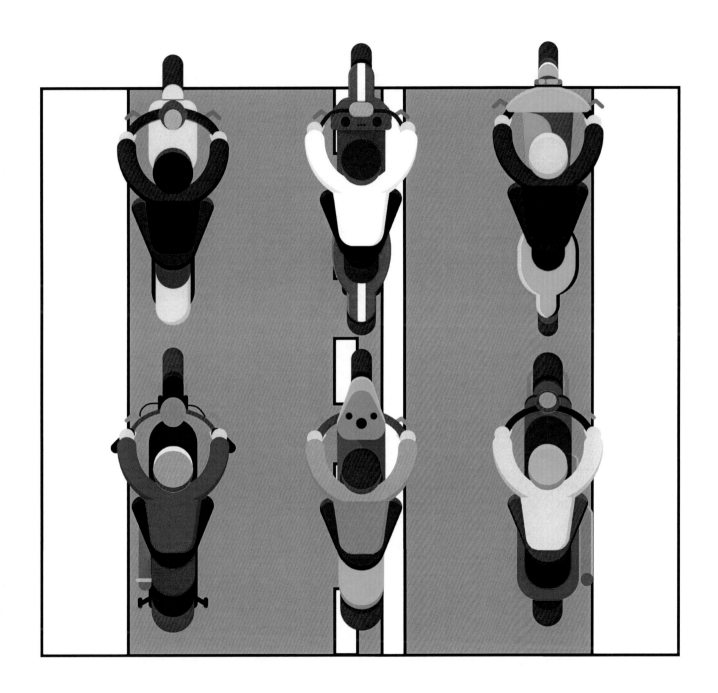

You can find all kinds of bikers in all kinds of places. One place you are sure to find them, is the Ice Cream shop!

There are a few things
that all riders like besides
ice cream.

Tacos and Puppies.

And they all like little kids.
If you ask nicely, they might let
you sit on their bike, or maybe
your grandpa will let you.

Made in United States
North Haven, CT
18 May 2023

36709949R00020